OUR BODY

Skeletal System

Cheryl Jakab

Smart Apple Media

Smart Apple Media
2140 Howard Drive West
North Mankato
Minnesota 56003

First published in 2006 by
MACMILLAN EDUCATION AUSTRALIA PTY LTD
627 Chapel Street, South Yarra, Australia 3141

Visit our Web site at www.macmillan.com.au

Associated companies and representatives throughout the world.

Library of Congress Cataloging-in-Publication Data

Jakab, Cheryl.
   The skeletal system / by Cheryl Jakab.
   p. cm. — (Our body)
   Includes index.
   ISBN-13: 978-1-58340-738-7
   1. Human skeleton—Juvenile literature. I. Title.

QM101.J22 2006
611'.71—dc22   2005057882

Edited by Ruth Jelley
Text and cover design by Peter Shaw
Illustrations by Guy Holt, Jeff Lang (p. 4 (bottom), pp. 5–6)
   and Ann Likhovetsky (p. 30)
Photo research by Legend Images

Printed in USA

Acknowledgments

The author and the publisher are grateful to the following for permission to reproduce copyright material:

Front cover photograph: Colored SEM/scanning electron micrograph of human spongy bone, courtesy of Photolibrary/Steve Gschmeissner/Science Photo Library.
Front cover illustration by Jeff Lang.

The DW Stock Picture Library, p. 22; Getty Images, p. 29; © Peter E. Smith, Natural Sciences Image Library, pp. 18, 24, 25, 27; Photodisc, pp. 14, 20; Photolibrary RF, p. 23; Photolibrary/Ifa-Bilderteam Gmbh, p. 28; Photolibrary/Science Photo Library, pp. 9 (all), 17, 26.

While every care has been taken to trace and acknowledge copyright, the publisher tenders their apologies for any accidental infringement where copyright has proved untraceable. Where the attempt has been unsuccessful, the publisher welcomes information that would redress the situation.

Contents

Glossary words
When a word is printed in **bold**, you can look up its meaning in the Glossary on page 31.

Amazing body structures

The human body is an amazing living thing. The structures of the body are divided into systems. Each system is made up of **cells**. Huge numbers of cells make up the **tissues** of the body systems. Each system performs a different, vital function. This series looks at six of the systems in the most familiar living thing to you—your body.

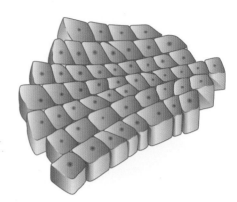

Cells make up tissues of the body systems.

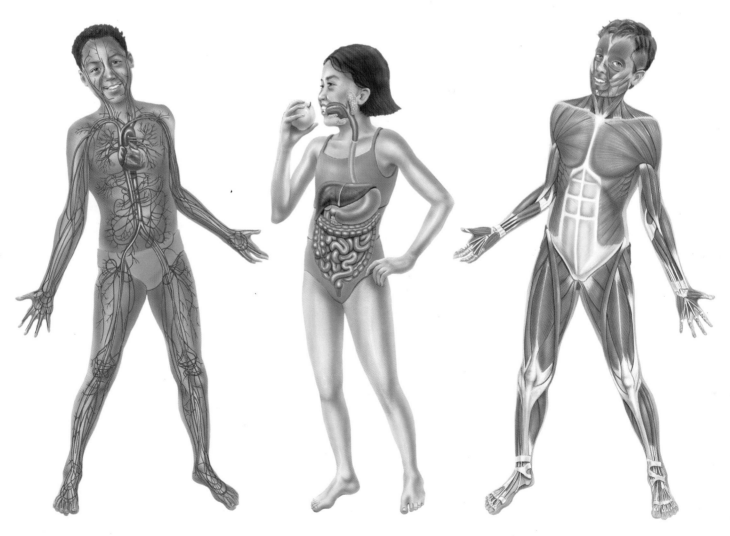

circulatory system   digestive system   muscular system

The skeletal system

The skeletal system is the hard framework that holds the body up.
How much do you know about your skeletal system?
- Do you know how many bones you have?
- Have you ever wondered what each bone does in your body?
- How do bones grow?
- What happens if you break a bone?

This book looks at the human skeletal system to answer these questions and more.

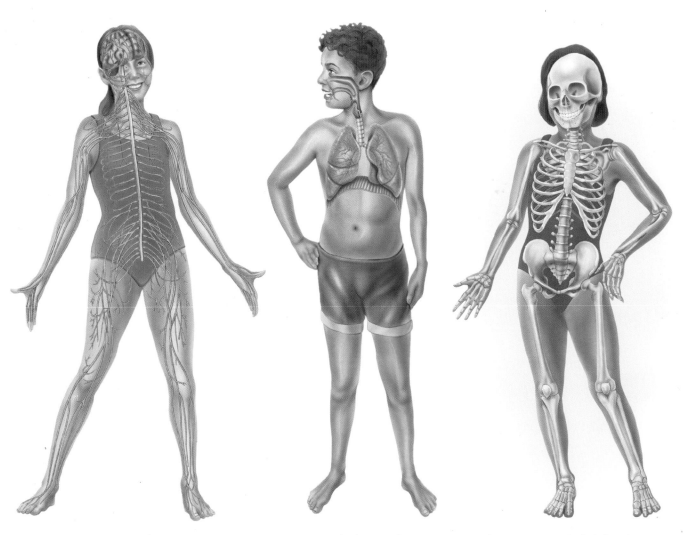

nervous system   respiratory system   skeletal system

Parts of the skeletal system

All the soft parts of the body, such as muscles, hang on the skeleton. Bones need to be strong and yet light. They must be strong to support the body, and light so they are easy to move. The 206 bones of the human skeleton are grouped into two main sections:

- the **axial skeleton**, or central column, which is made up of the skull, backbone (spine), and ribs
- the **appendicular skeleton**, or appendages, which are arms and legs that are attached to the central column

FASCINATING FACT

The actual number of bones in an adult body varies from one person to another. The average number is 206.

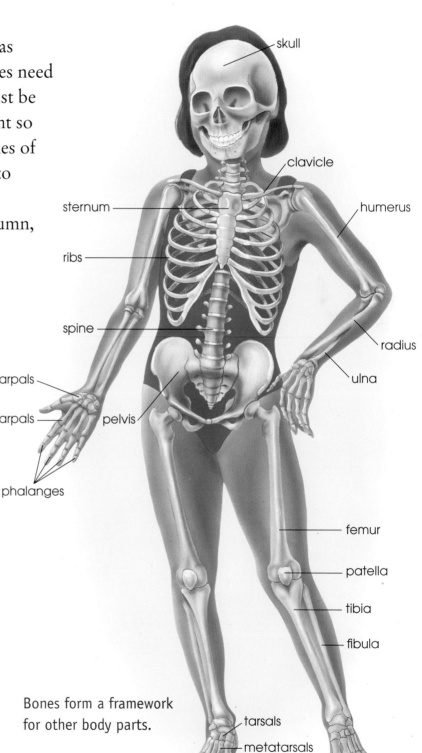

Bones form a framework for other body parts.

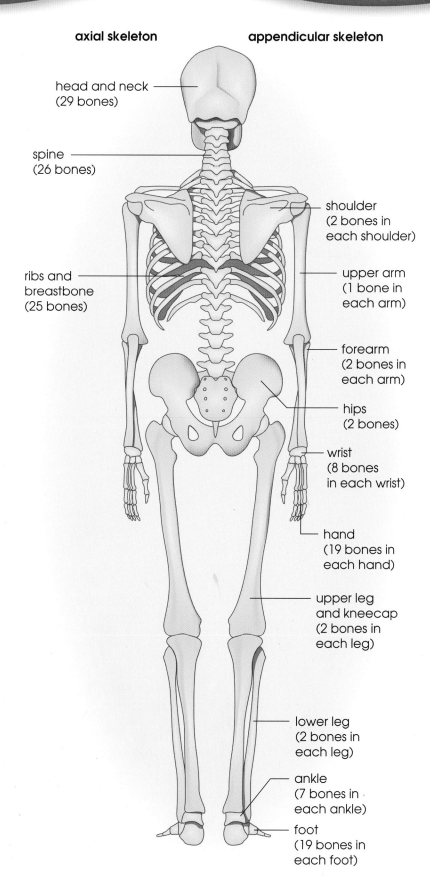

axial skeleton   appendicular skeleton

head and neck
(29 bones)

spine
(26 bones)

shoulder
(2 bones in
each shoulder)

ribs and
breastbone
(25 bones)

upper arm
(1 bone in
each arm)

forearm
(2 bones in
each arm)

hips
(2 bones)

wrist
(8 bones
in each wrist)

hand
(19 bones in
each hand)

upper leg
and kneecap
(2 bones in
each leg)

lower leg
(2 bones in
each leg)

ankle
(7 bones in
each ankle)

foot
(19 bones in
each foot)

Axial skeleton

The axial skeleton consists of 80 bones. There are eight bones in the skull, 13 in the face and upper jaw, and one in the lower jaw. There are a total of six tiny bones in the ears. There is one front neck bone (hyoid bone) and one **breastbone**. The spine consists of 26 bones and the ribs consist of 24 bones.

Appendicular skeleton

The appendicular skeleton consists of 126 bones. There are 32 bones in each arm, which is made up of two shoulder bones, three arm bones, eight wrist bones, and 19 bones in the hand and fingers. There is a total of 31 bones in each leg. Each leg has one hip bone, one upper leg bone, one kneecap bone, two lower leg bones, seven ankle bones, and 19 bones in the foot and toes.

The rear view of the skeleton clearly shows the shoulder blades and the points where the ribs meet the spine.

Layers of bone

Bones are made up of two hard outer layers (**compact bone** and **spongy bone**) and a soft inner layer. In many bones the inner layer consists of a Jell-O-like material called bone marrow, which makes blood cells.

Bones marrow can be found in long bones, such as the femur.

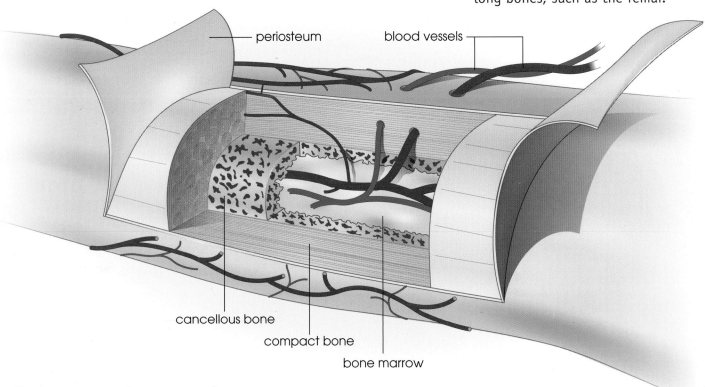

periosteum   blood vessels

cancellous bone

compact bone

bone marrow

Compact and spongy bone

Compact bone tissue is very dense and heavy. Inside the compact bone is a layer of spongy bone, called cancellous (say kan-sell-us) bone. Spongy bone tissue is not as hard as compact bone, but it is still very strong.

Periosteum

There is a thin membrane, called the periosteum (say pe-ree-os-tee-um), covering each bone. The periosteum contains nerves and blood vessels which nourish the bone.

TRY THIS

Look at a real bone

Get a fresh leg bone of a lamb or cow from the butcher. Ask the butcher to cut the bone in half. Look at the layers of bone. Is there any bone marrow inside the bone?

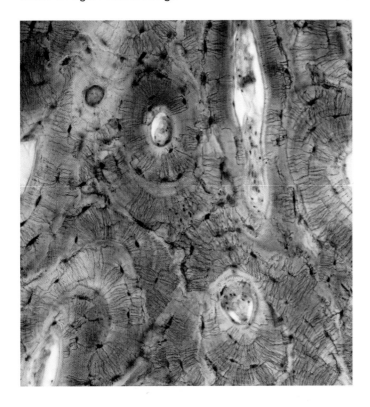

Bone tissue

Bone tissue is made up largely of **minerals**, water, and nutrients called carbohydrates. It is the minerals, particularly **calcium**, that make bones hard. The more calcium and other minerals in the bone tissue, the harder it is. Spongy bone is made of strands of bone tissue, like a framework with large gaps in between the strands. Compact bone is very hard and solid with few gaps in the bone tissue.

The strands of bone tissue in spongy bone make it light and strong.

Bone cells
UNDER THE MICROSCOPE

Bone cells, called osteocytes, sit in a tiny hole in the bone material called a lacuna (say lak-oo-nah). The bone material is called the matrix of bone.

Compact bone is made of solid bone material.

Bones of the skeleton

The bones of the skeleton have many different shapes. For example, leg bones are long and thin. Bones in the spine have projections (pointy bits). The shape of a bone is related to how it functions in the body.

Skull bones

The skull is made up of a number of bones. The skullcap, or cranium, is a set of thick bones that are **fused** together. There are eight bones in the cranium, which forms a protective covering over the brain.

The skull includes 14 bones that make up the face. All these bones are fixed in place except for the lower jaw, which moves when chewing or talking. The teeth are not counted as bones, because they are not made of bone tissue.

FASCINATING FACT
A baby's skull bones are separate and very soft. A baby's skull has a gap in the top called a fontanel. The skull bones fuse together after a child stops growing, leaving lines on the surface, called sutures.

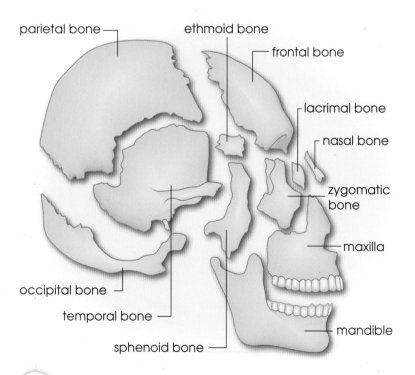

In total, there are 22 bones in the skull.

Hand and foot bones

Hand and foot bones are very similar. Even the name for the bones in the fingers and toes is the same. They are called the phalanges (say fa-lan-jeez). However, the thumb is different to any other part of the hands and feet. It has the ability to move in circles as well as back and forth. Thumbs are used to pick up and move objects.

HEALTH TIP

Foot care

Good footwear protects your feet and makes sure all the bones move correctly. Incorrectly fitted shoes can cause foot problems, such as calluses, or push bones out of place.

Tip: When buying shoes make sure you have them fitted correctly.

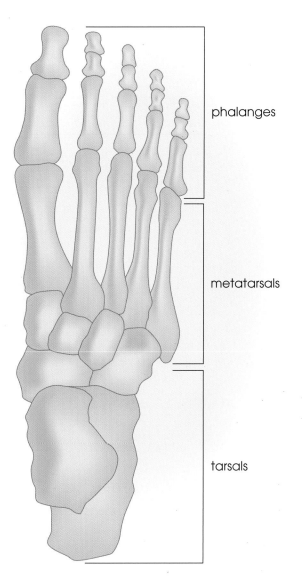

phalanges

metatarsals

tarsals

The ankle is made up of only seven tarsal bones.

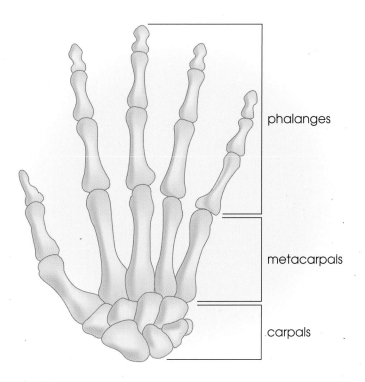

phalanges

metacarpals

carpals

The wrist is made up of eight carpal bones.

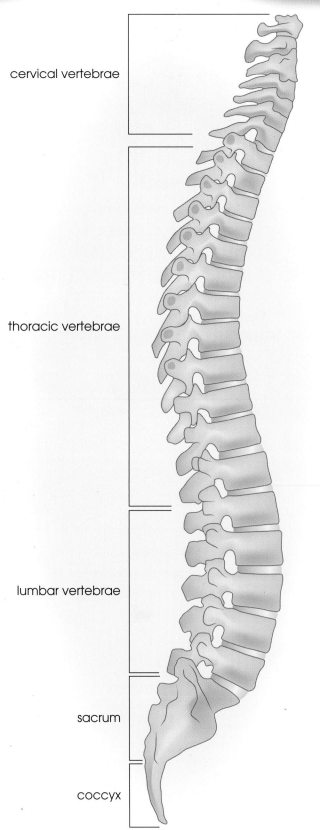

cervical vertebrae

thoracic vertebrae

lumbar vertebrae

sacrum

coccyx

The spine is made up of three sections of vertebrae and two sets of fused vertebrae.

The spine

The spine is the main structural support of the body. It is a column of ring-shaped bones called vertebrae (say vert-a-bray). The 33 vertebrae in the spine are divided into three groups. The cervical vertebrae in the upper spine support the head and neck. The thoracic vertebrae in the middle of the spine anchor the ribs. Lumbar vertebrae at the bottom of the spine are the largest and thickest. They provide the most support and stability. The **sacrum** and **coccyx** at the base of the spine are made of several vertebrae that are fused together.

Rib cage

There 12 pairs of ribs which create a cage around the chest to protect the heart and lungs inside. Each pair of ribs links to one vertebra.

FASCINATING FACT

Did you know that humans and giraffes have the same number of bones in their necks? The vertebrae in a giraffe's neck are much, much longer than a human's!

Bending and the spine

Together, the 33 vertebrae allow the spine to bend in many directions. It can bend forward and backward, and from side to side. If the spine was one long bone we would not be **flexible** at all.

Spine curves

A healthy spine curves slightly. From the side the spine can be seen to curve slightly forward at the neck, slightly backward at the chest, and slightly forward at the hips.

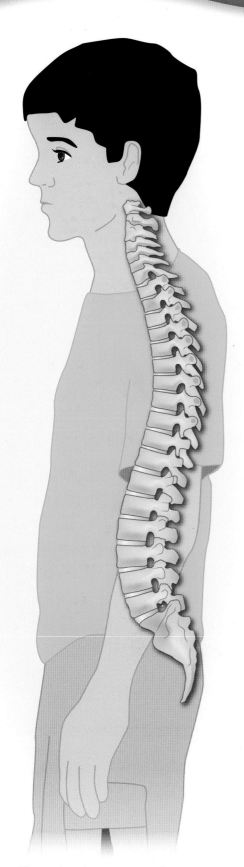

The spine has a natural curve.

HEALTH TIP
Back care

Chiropractors are health care professionals who move the joints in the spine to get the vertebrae into normal alignment.

Tip: Hanging by the arms or the legs for a few minutes each day is a good way to help vertebrae sit in the correct position.

Moving bones and joints

Wherever bones meet there are joints. Joints allow the body
to move in different ways. Some joints allow a wide range
of movements, while others are more fixed. The joints where
the appendages meet the axial skeleton have the widest range of
movements.

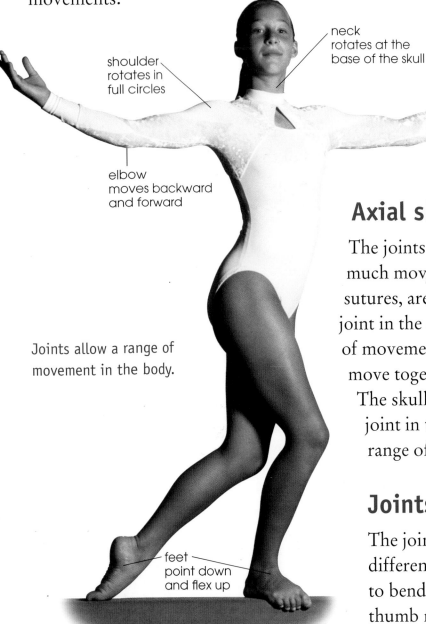

neck
rotates at the
base of the skull

thumb
rotates, moves backward
and forward

shoulder
rotates in
full circles

elbow
moves backward
and forward

Joints allow a range of
movement in the body.

feet
point down
and flex up

Axial skeleton joints

The joints in the axial skeleton do not have
much movement. The joints in the skull, the
sutures, are totally fixed. Each individual
joint in the spine allows only a limited range
of movement. However, when all these joints
move together, the spine is quite flexible.
The skull connection at the neck is the only
joint in the axial skeleton that has a wide
range of movements.

Joints in appendages

The joints in the appendages move in
different ways. The elbow allows the arm
to bend in the middle. The joint where the
thumb meets the wrist can rotate as well as
move forward, backward, and sideways.

Types of joints

There five types of joints which move in different ways.

A pivot joint, such as the top of the neck, allows the head to circle.

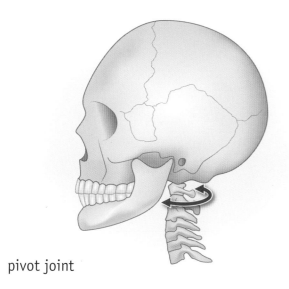

pivot joint

The shoulder joint is called a ball and socket joint. The rounded end of the arm bone fits into a socket in the shoulder. It allows the arm to move in a full circle.

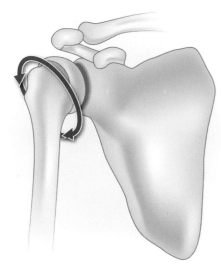

ball and socket joint

A hinge joint, such as the elbow, moves in one direction only, like a hinged door.

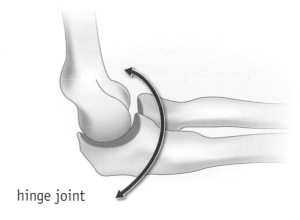

hinge joint

The thumb has a saddle joint that can rock back and forth and move side to side. The end of the metacarpal moves across the carpal, like a horse rider in a saddle.

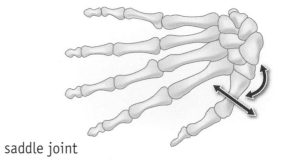

saddle joint

Feet have joints that allow the tarsals and metatarsals to glide over each other. The ends of the bones are almost flat where they meet.

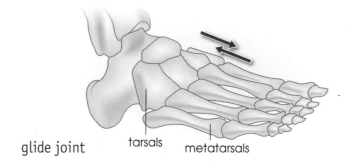

glide joint   tarsals   metatarsals

Cartilage in joints

Joints have cushioning in them, called **cartilage**. Cartilage tissue is similar to bone tissue but is softer and more flexible. Cartilage stops the hard ends of bones from rubbing together as they move. Without cartilage, the ends of bones would wear down quickly.

Cartilage also sits in the middle of some joints. Knees and vertebrae have this extra disc of cartilage, because these joints take a great deal of strain. These discs of cartilage help to absorb shock during activities such as running.

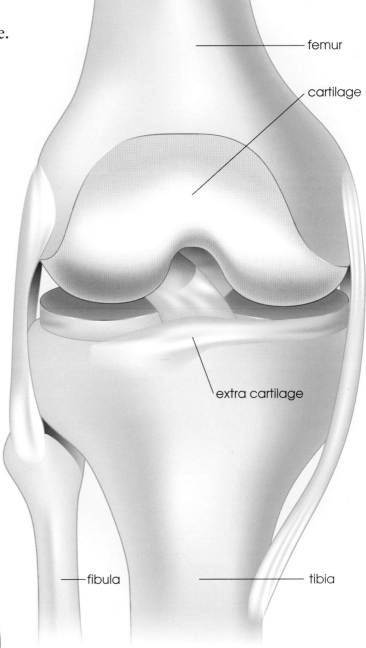

The knee joint has extra cartilage in the middle to protect it from shock.

HEALTH TIP
Knee care

Knee cartilage injuries are common in many sports where running and quick turns are combined. Knee joints take a great deal of strain in these activities.

Tip: Proper training and warm-ups can help prevent many injuries.

Cartilage in other parts of the body

Some body parts, including the ears, breastbone, and the windpipe, or trachea, have a cartilage framework. The outer part of the ear, called the pinna, is made of cartilage. It acts like a funnel to channel sound into the ear. The strong but moveable tissue that gives the nose its shape is made of cartilage. This flexible tip of cartilage protects the nasal bone.

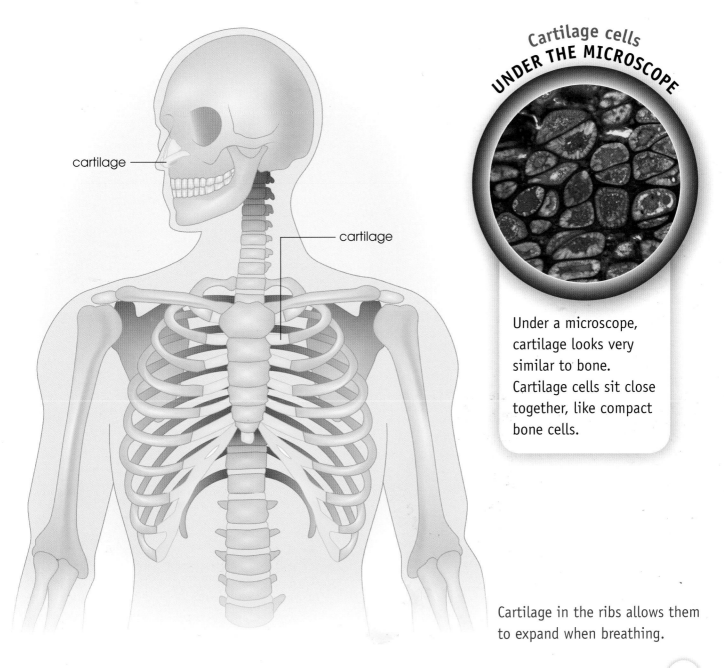

cartilage

cartilage

Cartilage cells UNDER THE MICROSCOPE

Under a microscope, cartilage looks very similar to bone. Cartilage cells sit close together, like compact bone cells.

Cartilage in the ribs allows them to expand when breathing.

Development of the skeleton

Bone growth occurs in the cartilage at the ends of bones. New bone is made when the soft cartilage grows and then hardens. This hardening of cartilage is called **ossification**. During ossification, calcium is added to the cartilage, which turns it into the harder bone tissue.

An unborn baby's skeleton is largely made of cartilage. Ossification occurs as the child develops. Bones become completely ossified in early adulthood. Once ossification is complete bones stop growing.

> **!**
>
> **FASCINATING FACT**
> As bones grow, the cartilage cells in the ends divide to produce more cells. The matrix then hardens to become bone.

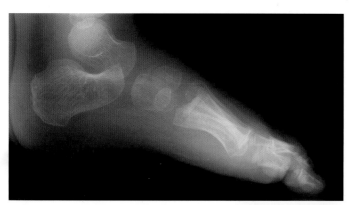

The bones in this child's foot are not fully developed, and consist mainly of cartilage.

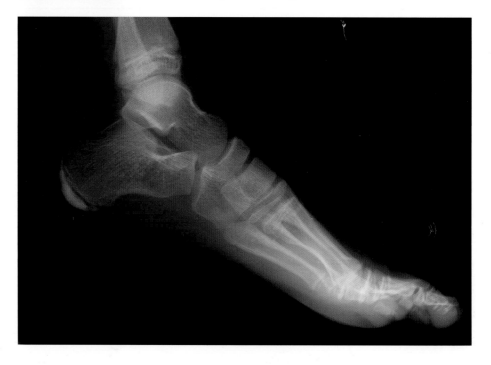

Once ossification is complete the bones are fully developed.

Growth from birth to adulthood

Babies are, on average, about 20 inches (50 cm) long when they are born, but they don't stay that small for long. Babies grow very quickly after birth as their bones develop and get longer. Growing slows as the baby gets older, but continues at a steady rate through childhood. Growing speeds up again during the teenage years. Full adult size is reached sometime after 16 years of age.

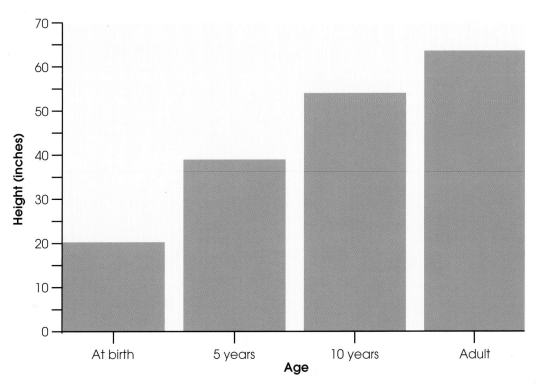

Long bone growth

Most of the growth in height during the teenage years is due to the lengthening of long bones in the legs and arms. The area of the bone where growth occurs is called the epiphysis (say e-pif-e-sis). The shaft of a long bone, such as the femur in the upper leg, gets longer only at the epiphysis.

FASCINATING FACT

A baby's head is about one quarter of the baby's total body length. In adults, the head is just one eighth of the overall height.

Body shapes and sizes

The size of a person's bones determines body characteristics, such as shape and height. The average height of an adult is about 5.5 feet (170 cm). Some adults are less than 3.3 feet (100 cm) tall, while others are more than 6.6 feet (200 cm) tall.

People are all different, but there are some general trends in body shape and size. Tall people have longer legs and arms. Short people are shorter in the **torso**, legs, and arms, and have small feet and hands.

Nutrition does affect overall body size, but genes inherited from parents are a greater influence. Small parents are likely to have smaller than average children. Tall parents are likely to have taller children.

TRY THIS

Body proportions

With a friend, cut a piece of string to match your height. Use a pen to mark the height of your shoulder, hip and knee on the string. Fold the string to work out your body proportions. How many leg lengths are there in your total body height?

People have a range of body shapes and sizes.

Male and female skeletons

Male and female skeletons differ in shape. The major difference between them is the shape of the pelvis. The pelvis is the fused ring of bones at the hip. It is designed to give support to the upper body and protect the **abdomen**. Adult men have a narrower pelvis than women. A female pelvis is wider and not as deep, to allow for childbirth.

The difference is visible after the teenage years when bone development is completed. Male and female skeletons also differ in height. On average, men are taller than women. A boy's rapid growth phase at puberty is generally later than a girl's. Boys reach their adult height slightly later than girls.

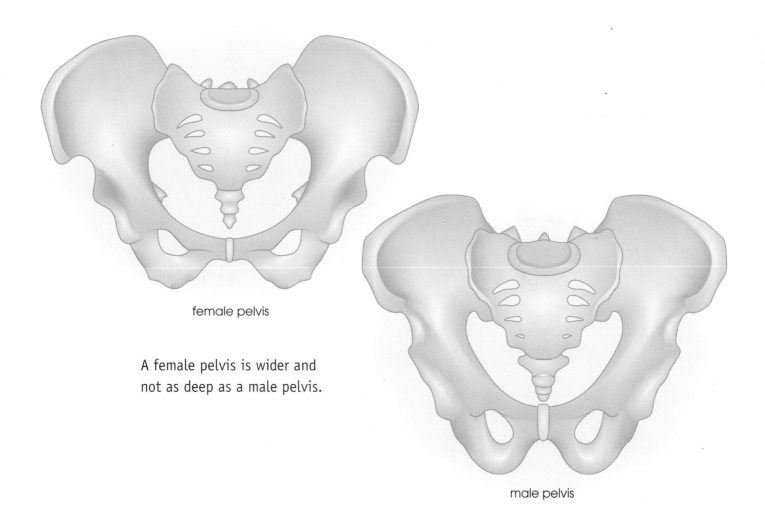

female pelvis

A female pelvis is wider and not as deep as a male pelvis.

male pelvis

Healthy bones

Strong, healthy bones are built by getting plenty of exercise and eating the right food. Many people today have an inactive lifestyle where they sit for much of the day. An inactive lifestyle is not very good for bones.

Exercise

Exercise encourages bones to take up more calcium, which makes them hard and strong. The best exercise for healthy bones is known as weight-bearing exercise. In weight-bearing exercise, such as running, the bones carry the body's weight. It has been shown that weight-bearing exercise increases the strength of bones more than other forms of exercise.

Weight-bearing exercise helps to develop strong bones.

✚ HEALTH TIP
Get active

If your lifestyle involves very little physical activity, you have a greater risk of having weak bones that lack calcium.

Tip: Jumping with two feet together is a great weight-bearing exercise.

Diet

A diet rich in calcium is needed for strong bone growth and to keep bones hard. Vitamin D is also required, as it controls the absorption of calcium from food. We get most of our vitamin D from exposure to sunlight. Some vitamin D can be found in foods such as eggs, fish, and liver. It is best to get a dose of sunlight each day to help your body use the calcium in your diet.

HEALTH TIP
Calcium intake
The recommended daily intake of calcium for children aged 8 to 11 years is 0.032 ounces (900 mg) for girls, and 0.028 ounces (800 mg) for boys.

Tip: Try non-dairy sources of calcium, including broccoli, tofu, dried beans, and shellfish.

Calcium-rich foods

Foods that are rich in calcium include milk, cheese, yoghurt, broccoli, tofu, oranges, and dried beans and peas. However, the body absorbs calcium more easily from some sources than others. Each person needs to find calcium-rich foods that they can eat.

Dried beans are a good source of calcium.

Bone problems

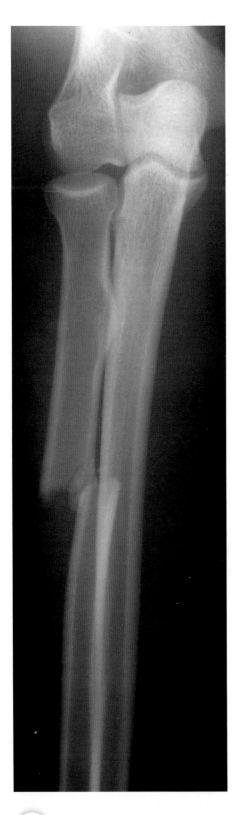

This X ray shows a break in the forearm bone (radius) near the elbow joint.

Bone problems, such as breaks and **genetic disorders**, can affect people of all ages. **Fractures** are among the most common injuries suffered by children. Scientists continue to research the causes and effects of bone damage and find treatments.

Fractures

Forceful knocks and falls can cause bone fractures. Fractures range from tiny cracks, or fissures, to breaks right through the bone. A fractured bone in a healthy body will heal after a few weeks.

Osteoporosis

Osteoporosis (say os-tee-oh-por-oh-sis) occurs when bones lose calcium. Bones become weak and are more easily fractured. Lack of exercise and low calcium levels can lead to osteoporosis at any age. Severe osteoporosis sufferers become shorter and many develop a hunchback.

FASCINATING FACT

A severe lack of vitamin D in children can lead to a disease called rickets, which causes deformities in new bones. Evidence of rickets has been found in the ancient bones dug up by archeologists.

Joint problems

Common joint problems include ligament and cartilage tears, dislocations, and arthritis.

Dislocation

Dislocation occurs when bones are pulled out from their normal positions. Ligaments, which help hold joints together, become damaged along with nerves and blood vessels. Dislocated joints look badly out of shape and cause swelling and severe pain.

Arthritis

Arthritis occurs when joints become swollen and painful. The most common form of arthritis is osteoarthritis (say os-tee-oh-arth-ry-tis). This occurs when the cartilage in joints begins to break down. Cartilage normally wears away as the body ages, so most people suffer some arthritis by about 60 years of age.

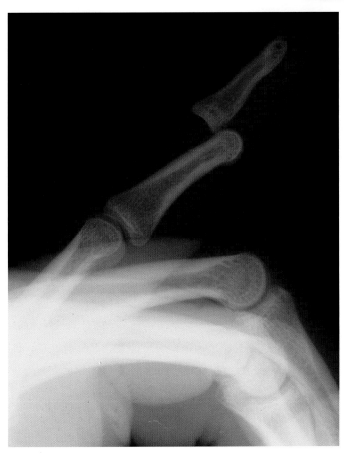

This X ray shows a dislocated phalanx (finger bone).

HEALTH TIP
Young children's joints

Young children's elbow or shoulder joints can be easily dislocated if their arm is pulled too hard.

Tip: Pick up toddlers and babies around their torso, not by their arms.

Treating problems

Doctors are able to look inside the body using medical imaging tools such as X rays. Bone scans can be used to show how solid a bone is.

X rays

X ray images show shadows of structures inside the body. Very dense tissue, such as bone, shows up on X rays more than softer tissues, such as cartilage. X rays are most commonly used to diagnose bone and joint disorders.

FASCINATING FACT

X ray is the oldest form of medical imaging. X rays were discovered in 1895. Within a few months of their discovery, X rays were being used to diagnose bone fractures.

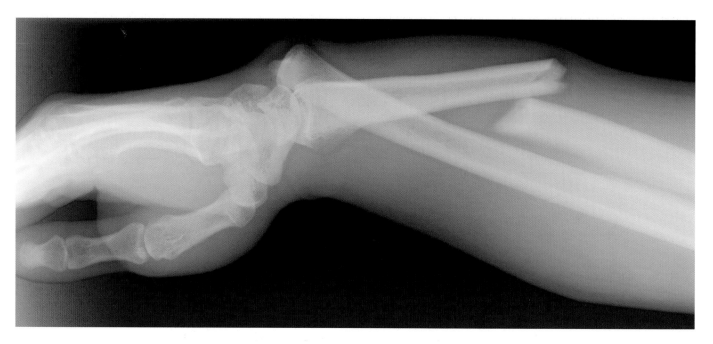

This X ray shows a broken radius and dislocation of the ulna at the wrist.

Bone density scans

Bone scans can help show if bone density, or solidity, is normal. Healthy bones consist of 65 to 70 percent minerals, such as calcium. Women over 50 years of age are at high risk of losing calcium and should have their bone density checked regularly.

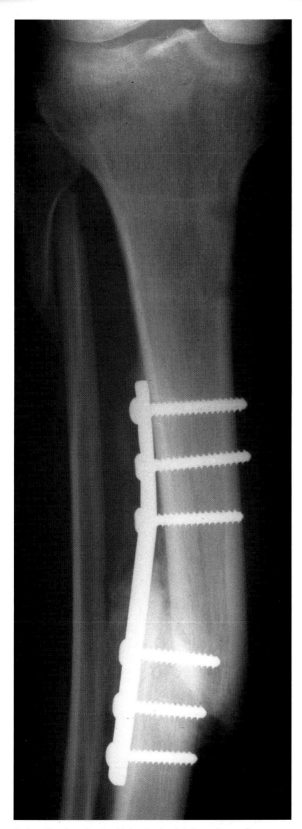

A badly broken tibia is held in place by a metal plate and several screws.

Pins and screws

Screws, pins, nails, nuts, and bolts are often used in surgery to repair badly broken bones. Sometimes when breaks are severe or do not heal well, doctors assist the healing process by pinning the bones together. Pins and screws are made of metal. The experts who conduct the surgery to insert them are called orthopedic surgeons. Sometimes the pins and screws are left in place permanently. Sometimes they are removed after the bones have healed.

Artificial joints

Artificial joints are sometimes used to replace severely damaged joints. Hip joint replacement is now a very successful treatment for older people.

HEALTH TIP
Back care

Spine problems are among the most common bone problems. They can lead to spinal curvatures and foot and neck problems. Learning to lift heavy items correctly will help prevent injury.

Tip: Keep your back straight and bend your knees when picking up heavy objects.

Taking care of bones

Falling over when playing can cause bones to break. Broken bones are painful and healing takes time. Taking some simple precautions can prevent injuries from occurring.

Safety gear

When riding a bike, protect your skull and brain by wearing a correctly fitted safety helmet. Skateboarders and rollerbladers should also wear padding to protect joints, such as knees, wrists, and elbows.

The right exercise

Weight-bearing exercise helps to build strong bones. However, continual high-pressure work, such as professional sports training, can cause "stress" fractures. The growing bones of children can be at risk of stress fractures if they are overworked.

Wearing safety gear provides protection from injury when rollerblading.

HEALTH TIP
Strength and flexibility

Stretching and weight-bearing exercises strengthen bones and make joints flexible, which helps to reduce injury.
Tip: Take yoga classes to develop strength and flexibility.

Follow safety advice

It is great to be active and use your body, but all games involve risks. Some activities, such as backflips, are high-risk and can cause severe damage. If you want to do high-risk activities, you need to learn them in a safe environment with adult supervision.

In case of emergency

If you are nearby when someone is injured, you should:

- stay calm
- ask what hurts
- keep the injured person comfortable, but do not move them
- seek medical assistance.

Be prepared

It is important to be prepared for emergencies. Learn emergency service numbers and practice what to ask for (police, ambulance, or fire services). In the United States, emergency services are contacted by dialing 911.

Gymnastics practice should always be supervised by an adult.

ACTIVITY Make a bone bend

You can make a bone bendable by taking the calcium out of it using an acid, such as vinegar. This leaves soft cartilage behind.

You will need

- a fresh, uncooked chicken bone
- a jug
- white vinegar

What to do

1 Place the chicken bone in the jug.

2 Pour white vinegar over the bone until it is completely covered.

3 After three days, tip the vinegar out and pour in fresh vinegar.

4 Repeat this every three days, for three weeks.

5 After three weeks, wash the rubbery bone. It should now bend easily, as all the calcium has been removed.

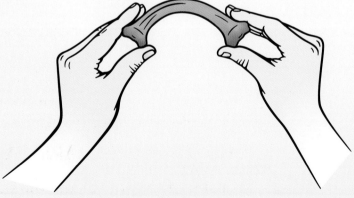

Glossary

abdomen	the area below the chest
appendicular skeleton	the part of the skeleton which is made up of the bones in the arms and legs, which are attached to the axial skeleton
axial skeleton	the central part of the skeleton that is made up of the skull, spine, and ribs
breastbone	the bone that connects the collarbone to the ribs, also called the sternum
calcium	mineral found in bones
cartilage	tough bendy material at the ends of bones
cells	smallest unit of living things
coccyx	the very end of the spine which sits below the sacrum, also called the tailbone
compact bone	the hard outer layer of a bone
flexible	able to bend
fractures	broken bones that may be cracked, broken right through, or shattered
fused	joined together permanently
genetic disorders	disorders that are inherited, or passed on in a family from one generation to the next
minerals	chemicals with a crystal structure that make bones hard
ossification	the process of cartilage hardening to form bone
sacrum	the fused vertebrae at the bottom of the spine which connect to the pelvis
spongy bone	the hard layer of bone inside the compact bone
tissues	groups of similar cells which make up the fabric of body systems
torso	the trunk of the body, from the shoulders down to the buttocks

Index